TO

FROM

DATE

ONE MORE DAY

STEVEN DALE JONES, BOBBY TOMBERLIN, AND DIAMOND RIO

Rutledge Hill Press™

Nashville, Tennessee

A Division of Thomas Nelson, Inc.

www.ThomasNelson.com

Published by Rutledge Hill Press, a division of Thomas Nelson, Inc., P.O. Box 141000, Nashville,
Tennessee 37214

Scripture quotations are taken from *The Living Bible*, copyright © 1971. Used by permission of
Tyndale House Publishers, Inc., Wheaton, IL 60189 USA. All rights reserved.

Design: Lookout Design Group, Inc., Minneapolis, Minnesota

ISBN: 1-4016-0007-7

Printed in the United States of America

02 03 04 05 06 --- 5 4 3 2 1

We dedicate this book to our families.

—STEVE AND BOBBY

INTRODUCTION

It's so easy to get caught up in the immediate—our jobs, our appointments, our obligations. It's equally easy to disregard the important—our families, our friends, our passions. Today's world can spin faster than our ability to make a difference.

It is our hope, through music, lyrics, testimony, and observation, that *One More Day* will heighten your times of joy and bring comfort to your times of overwhelming sadness, leading us all to *make every day count.*

—DIAMOND RIO

ONE MORE DAY

Last night I had a crazy dream

A wish was granted just for me

It could be for anything

I didn't ask for money

Or a mansion in Malibu

I simply wished for one more day with you

One more day, one more time

One more sunset, maybe I'd be satisfied

But then again, I know what it would do

Leave me wishing still, for one more day with yo

First thing I'd do is pray for time to crawl

Then I'd unplug the telephone

And keep the TV off

I'd hold you every second

Say a million "I love you's"

That's what I'd do with one more day with you

One more day, one more time

One more sunset, maybe I'd be satisfied

But then again, I know what it would do

Leave me wishing still, for one more day with you

THE SUNRISE...

Get up before it does.

CELEBRATE EVERY MOMENT!

Today will **NEVER** pass your way again. Live it like there's **NO TOMORROW.**

If you're like me, you spend way too
much time with the past.
Why do we waste the precious moments of today on things
that are over our shoulder?

We can't change it.

We can't relive it.

If you're like me, you spend way too much time
contemplating the future.
Why do we waste the precious moments of today on things
that may never happen?

TODAY IS **IMPORTANT**.
TODAY **MATTERS**.

"A day without laughter is a day wasted."
– CHARLIE CHAPLIN

EACH DAY

is a gift and
a blessing

SENT OUR WAY.

1 DAY...

24 Hours...

1,440 minutes...

86,400 seconds . . .

► JUST THINK OF THE DIFFERENCE
YOU CAN MAKE IN THAT AMOUNT OF TIME.

If I knew I only had **ONE MORE DAY** with you,

I'd *breathe* you into my soul.

I'd *fill* my heart and mind with you.

I'd *hang* on every word you said and bury,

deep inside my memory, the sound of your voice.

"TAKE A PAUSE AND ENJOY THE DAY AND THE PEOPLE YOU HAVE BEEN GIVEN IN LIFE. THEY ARE TRULY A BLESSING."

MARTY ROE
DIAMOND RIO

FORGIVE...

God does it all the time.

WHAT MAKES US
THINK WE SHOULDN'T?

We should cherish every day

we are given with the ones we love.

We don't know if we will ever have

ONE MORE DAY.

Let's make sure we kiss before we say good-bye.

If I only had ONE MORE DAY,

I'd let my kids tell me what to do.

When the kids spill Coke on the kitchen floor,

When they play their music a little too loud,

When they tie up the telephone for hours,

When they leave their bedroom in a mess,

And just when you're about to lose your cool,

IMAGINE HOW EMPTY YOUR HOME AND

LIFE WOULD BE WITHOUT THEM.

Hey guys!

You're never too old to give your dad a hug.

For years I looked forward to my senior
year in high school and graduation day.

I've also spent years looking back on it.
Live every day of it . . .
Breathe it in deeper . . .
Open your eyes wider . . .
And try to remember every moment.

–SDJ

"Dream as if you'll live forever.
Live as if you'll die today."

—JAMES DEAN

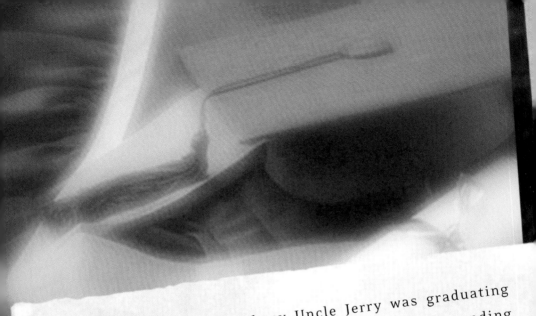

The year was 1970 and my Uncle Jerry was graduating from high school. I was all of four years old and spending the day with my grandparents, and I'll never forget my grandmother walking back into the house from checking the mail. I can still see the fear on her face as she handed my uncle a letter from the U.S. Marines. He had enlisted to go to Vietnam and the papers had arrived letting him know he would be leaving. Even though I was too young to understand, I could feel the fear everyone else was feeling.

I remember everyone saying good-bye, not knowing if we would ever see him again. I can still see my grandparents waiting for the mailman and praying for a letter from their youngest son. After a couple of years, he came home—safe. We were so proud. I can't imagine what he went through. After eighteen years of safe country living, church on Sunday, Mama's home-cooking, drive-in movies, and then having to go to a land so far away and fight in a war, hanging on second to second, you can bet he appreciates having ONE MORE DAY.

—BT

TIME WAITS FOR NO ONE.

So why should you?

"How do you know what is going to happen tomorrow? For the length of your lives is as uncertain as the morning fog—now you see it; soon it is gone."

— JAMES 4:14

Dear Paige,

As you're getting ready to walk down those high school halls for the last time, STOP. Go and say thanks to that first grade teacher who was patient while you learned to spell. Tell the cooks thanks for twelve years of meals. Remember that first crush, the cheerleading camps, driving onto campus for the first time after getting your driver's license, your first prom, and enjoy the drive to and from school with your sister because you will never experience moments like these again. Also, remember that classmate whose life ended way too soon in that terrible accident. And as you get ready to take a bigger leap in this thing called life, promise to stay in touch with your friends. I pray when you come back for your ten-year class reunion, life will have treated you well.

—BT

LIFE IS
BITTERSWEET
...CONCENTRATE ON THE
SWEET.

DANA WILLIAMS
DIAMOND RIO

LIFE IS FRAGILE.
HANDLE **WITH CARE.**

It was a weekend senior trip to the beach in
Panama City, Florida.

I ventured out a little too far in the ocean.

I was caught in an undertow.

I could just feel life slipping away.

But God wasn't ready for me.

I made it back to shore. I lived. Oh how I've
lived since then.

I've been accused of living five days in one.

—BT

I EXPERIENCED THE REGRET OF NOT HAVING SAID AND DONE ALL THE THINGS I SHOULD HAVE AND WOULD HAVE FOR THE TWO PEOPLE WHO HAD MY UNDYING, UNCONDITIONAL LOVE . . . MY PARENTS. WHAT COULD BE WORSE THAN NOT TELLING YOUR PARENTS HOW GRATEFUL YOU ARE FOR THEIR LOVE AND SUPPORT?

GENE JOHNSON

DIAMOND RIO

I could not ask for a better mom and dad. They adopted me when I was three months old. That's powerful love when someone can take a child that's not their own and dedicate their life to loving and caring for it. We live five hours apart, but I try to make the most of the time when we're together, whether it's going to church or just having lunch at the local café in my three-stoplight hometown.

The longer I live the more I realize that THE LITTLE THINGS SOMETIMES TURN OUT TO BE THE BIGGEST THINGS.

CHERISH THOSE TIMES WITH MOM AND DAD.

—BT

Dear God,

Help me understand and
appreciate the brevity of life.

IT'S NEVER TOO LATE
to call an old friend.

As far back as I can remember, all I ever wanted was to be involved in music. When I was five, my Uncle Robert and Uncle James, the family musicians, started showing me chords on the guitar. I was always so excited to see Uncle James and learn new chords and arrangements. As I grew older, I didn't see him as much but we'd try to get together around Christmas. On December 21 of 1994, he suffered an aneurysm and passed away suddenly. He and my aunt had called me a few weeks before and left a message inviting me to come visit. I was so wrapped up in my work, I had not even returned the call. His passing made me realize the importance of each day.

—BT

I asked a friend who plays in another band, "Why do you fly home so much instead of just riding the bus?" His response was, "there is always a chance to make more money, but there is only so much time."

—*Jimmy Olander,* DIAMOND RIO

What good is a million dollars if you don't have one more day?

IT'S NEVER TOO LATE
to mend a fence.

IT'S NEVER TOO LATE
to say, "I'm sorry."

GOD GIVES US WHAT WE NEED TO GET THROUGH HARD TIMES.

GENE JOHNSON
DIAMOND RIO

"Our lives begin to end the day we

become silent about things that matter."

—MARTIN LUTHER KING, JR.

We often hear the saying,
"make a difference in a life."

Each time I hear this, several
people come to mind who have
made a difference in mine.

I'm not even sure they know it.
That's my fault. I need to tell
them and thank them

TODAY.

The other day I called a good friend of mine who has been living with a life-threatening illness for years. He is now on a waiting list for a liver transplant.

Some people have, in the past, accused him of being too anxious, of trying too hard, of trying to do too much. He was only doing all he could to make each day count.

Wouldn't we all?
Shouldn't we all?

Just before I hung up he asked me my blood-type. I told him I didn't know.

He said he's going to need B-positive.

—SDJ

P.S. Yesterday he got a new liver. So far, so good.

Oh by the way!
DON'T BE AFRAID TO DREAM.

Throw in some faith and there's no telling
where you're dreams will take you.

This past year my Dad went to the doctor for his annual checkup. He thought he had a minor complication but after undergoing some tests, the doctor discovered he had cancer and if he didn't have immediate surgery, he wouldn't live another year. I'll never forget the sick feeling that came over me when my mom told me the doctor's report.

Surgery was a complete success and he continues to heal and is enjoying life more than ever. Hardly a day goes by now that I don't call to tell him and my Mom how much I love them.

—BT

We all know our days are numbered

BUT SOMETIMES

I FORGET

And I live like I'm
guaranteed forever
WHEN TOMORROW
AIN'T HERE YET.

There's a lady in a nursing home in Montgomery, Alabama, who said recently, "If I had my life to live over again, I would go fishing more. How I loved the feel of a catfish tugging on the fishing line. I would listen more closely to the birds singing. Now I can hardly hear it thunder even with this old hearing aid. I would visit my son and his wife in New York City instead of expecting them to come to me. I bet Times Square at Christmas is really something. I would go with my church group to the Grand Canyon. At the time I didn't want to ask for an extra three days off from work. My advice is to live and LIVE WELL WHILE YOU CAN."

*Nursing homes have
long visiting hours.*

A DAY WELL SPENT

I recently heard about an elderly
lady in her eighties who spends a
day each week at the local
nursing home, singing
and playing the piano
for the patients.

MY NINETY-THREE-YEAR-OLD
GRANDMOTHER AGREES THAT
LIFE IS SHORT.

Lessie Stephenson lived to be one hundred years old. For the last three years of her life, her roommate in a nursing home suffered from Alzheimer's and didn't know day from night. Mrs. Stephenson's family asked if she would like to change rooms and have a roommate with a sound mind. She quickly replied, "NO! I can't leave her—she needs me!"

No matter how old or young, we can make a difference as long as we have one more day.

"LIFE IS WHAT HAPPENS WHEN
YOU'RE BUSY MAKING OTHER PLANS."
–JOHN LENNON

DON'T
save it for a rainy day.

"Don't let the sun go down

with you still angry."

– EPHESIANS 4:26

IT'S NEVER TOO LATE
to say "I Love You."

TODAY. . .

DO SOMETHING YOU *WANT* TO DO,

NOT SOMETHING YOU **SHOULD** DO.

TODAY is the day I'm sending my mother flowers.

I'm going to call her and just listen as she talks.

I'm going to laugh at her jokes.

I'm going to seek her advice.

I'm going to thank her for my life.

I'm going to tell her I love her.

I'm going to do this TODAY.

ONE WINTER, A FIERCE ICE STORM
STRANDED MY WIFE AND ME AT HOME.
WE SPENT THOSE DAYS MAKING FIRES
AND DRINKING HOT CHOCOLATE.
I MAY HAVE TO PRETEND TO
GET STRANDED THIS WEEK!

JIMMY ORLANDER
DIAMOND RIO

Before the sun sets today, I'm going to

THE SUNSET. . .
Thank God for it.

GOD BLESS YOU AND MAY HE GRANT YOU ONE MORE DAY.

MARTY ROE

DIAMOND RIO

GENE JOHNSON

"One More Day" had been a number-one country song, and was currently in the top ten on the pop chart, when my daughter told me she had cancer. I finally understood that "One More Day" wasn't about what I *should have* said and done, but what I could say and do. My daughter is now cancer free and I am closer than ever to both of my daughters. God has granted me one more day.

MARTY ROE

Following the release of "One More Day," we began to hear very poignant stories of how the song had touched so many lives . . . from causing a parent to rededicate himself to his son, to comforting people in a loss of a loved one.

"One More Day" has given me renewed excitement about what I do. There are many people out there who have the same hopes and desires for the world as I do. I am so thankful to have been part of such a great message.

DAN TRUMAN

We had no idea of the impact this song would have on the hearts and lives of so many people. I don't go through one single day now without someone at the grocery store, a ball game, or just along the street thanking us for recording this song.

BRIAN PROUT

I've always known that God gives us but one day to live, but it wasn't until we recorded "One More Day" that I began to realize just how significant and powerful that attitude can be. It's my goal to cherish each new day and just make the most of it.

JIMMY OLANDER

"One More Day" has made me more aware of how precious and fragile our time is. You will see me taking advantage of the day I am given and protecting what I hold dear.

DANA WILLIAMS

It is my wish that this song, in whatever way, can continue to bless and minister to people . . . through good times and bad.